Hurt Into Beauty

Poems by
Paul Hostovsky

FutureCycle Press

Mineral Bluff, Georgia

Published by FutureCycle Press
Mineral Bluff, Georgia, USA

ISBN 978-0-9839985-9-4

Contents

For Marlene

The Violence of the Violins

It was in them, they would say.
It was what they were, what they
did. It was part of them, carved
into them like an F hole, like
a clef tattooed onto a biceps.
And there was nothing you
could say or do to change that.
It was their way. It was the way
of the world, and also of the sun
exploding a million miles away,
warming your soft cheek. Face
the music, they would say. Stop
listening with your eyes closed.
See the string tightened almost
to breaking, the bow torturing it
into song. Feel the skin stretched
over the drum so tightly it makes
your heart pound. And where
did you think it all came from,
the easy melody, the high tinkling
finery? We are hurt into beauty.
And you, up in the balcony, rising
to your feet, applauding fiercely, look
down at what your own hands are doing.

The Names

I want to say something about the names—
Ahmed, Fuad, Tarek, Toufic—
that are in the news these days—
Yusif, Anwar, Umar, Ismael—
and the way the newscasters have had
to practice pronouncing them. Abdul, Amar, Abu,
Muqtada al-Sadr. Don't you just
love saying, "Muqtada al-Sadr"?
If you lined up all the names and just
said them, one after the other,
it would sound like you were fluent
in Arabic. You could pull one over
on your friends down at the pub:
lubricate your tongue with a few beers,
then turn to Geoff or Bill or Steve, and say,
"Muqtada al-Sadr Ahmed Fuad
Abdul Abu Umar Muhammed," and just
wait for a reaction. Chances are
a painful silence would swallow the pub whole,
because everyone would think you had been praying,
or reciting a poem, or a fatwa, when in fact
all you were doing was saying the names,
just lining them up and one by one
firing off those frighteningly beautiful names.

Concentration Camps

The way I explained it to myself, the way
I made sense of it in my own way (I was eight
when I first learned about them), was all those people
starving and crying and dying together in those big
piles behind the barbed wire—were forced to concentrate
on suffering. So it made sense to call it that. That part
made sense, I thought, because concentration was very
difficult. And I hated having to do it myself
in elementary school when the teacher caught us
looking out the window at the trees, or the sky, or the rooftops
of the houses across the street—when she caught us looking
out at life—and forced us cruelly back to the problem
under our noses, the problem of the numbers, the problem
that wasn't going away no matter how much we
looked away from it. And those people, I thought, they must have
tried looking away from it too. They must have groaned
and looked away, and there must have been sky
above them, and trees on the other side, and maybe even a red
rooftop or two off in the distance where life was going on
in rooms with clean white linen and tinkling forks and knives . . .
The way you make sense of a problem like that,
a solution like that, a number like that, a number that's so big
you can't fit it in your head, can't fit it
in the world—though the world keeps trying that solution,
over and over—is to break it down, like the teacher said,
and keep breaking it down until you get to the smallest parts,
the ones divisible only by themselves and one: sky, tree, house,
one little boy. Then look out the window at the world again,
and see if it looks any different.

The First Day

They found the perpetrators.
The ones who committed those unspeakable acts.
Acts that were so unspeakable
they were all over the news,
so we all heard about them
and could only cover our mouths
and wonder how such people could do such things.
They found them, and they arrested them,
and they tried them and found them guilty. And the judge,
who was a very wise judge,
pronounced sentence: Begin again.
They must all begin again. Go back
and learn again the things we learned as children,
things they either never learned in the first place
or else somehow unlearned in the unspeakable
unforgiving place the world has always been
and will always be.
Things about being
with other people, about sharing, and keeping
your hands to yourself,
and laying your head down on your desk
in the crook of your elbow.
And so they were remanded
to kindergarten, each to a different
kindergarten, so they couldn't sit next to each other
and scoff, and keep each other from learning.
On the first day
each was brought in in shackles
before the bell rang,
and made to sit in one of the tiny desks,
so his knees came up to his chin. And when the children arrived
they noticed him right away, and gathered around him
timidly, curiously, a few emboldened to ask
questions, the kinds of questions only children

will ask: Are those real handcuffs? Are you
our new teacher? Are you Miss Butler's boyfriend?
And one of them climbed up into his lap, and one of them
rested a small hand on his huge shoulder,
and one, a girl, gazed up long and searchingly
into his dark, flitting, downcast eyes.

Clutch Steal

"This John Havlicek, he is Czech,"
says my father who is Czech
and doesn't speak English all that well
and doesn't know what a lay-up is, or a free-throw,
or a pick. We are sitting on the paisley couch,
watching the Celtics play the 76ers. It's 1965.
I hate to tell him, I tell him
as I steal the bag of potato chips from him,
but John Havlicek isn't Czech.
He's from Ohio. Born and raised. My father
was visiting someone in Belgium
when the Nazis invaded Czechoslovakia—
someone who set a pick for him, someone
who saw it all coming—and he escaped
to Paris, then to Lisbon, then to Oslo,
then to New York. Always one step ahead.
He was lucky. He was more than lucky.
He was—what's the word in English?—
charmed. And he lived. He lived, unlike his own
father, and mother, and brothers and sisters—his entire
team. All lost by the time that nightmare
was over. Twenty years later, he's sitting with me
on a paisley couch in a house in New Jersey,
watching the Celtics play the 76ers,
the announcer's impossible English sprinkled
with Havliceks: "Havlicek for two." "Havlicek
from the corner." "Havlicek under the boards."
And then John Havlicek steals the ball—
a clutch steal in the closing seconds of that game,
clinching the Eastern Conference Championship
and immortalizing Havlicek forever. My father
steals the potato chips back and says, "I am
liking this John Havlicek. He is maybe
from Ohio. But he is Czech. And he is charmed."

The Giving Tree

My Aunt Hannah taught 2nd grade.
And after the first amputation
which was only one toe
on her left foot, she came
to school carrying a silver cane,
and she let the kids use it
as a prop in their little skits,
and as a stickball bat at recess,
and to reach up into the tree
to rescue the kite. And the kids
were happy. But after the second
and third and fourth amputations—
this little piggy and his neighbor,
then the whole damn block, then up to the knee,
and then a year later all over again
on the other side of the street—
the kids had a different teacher.
And my Aunt Hannah came to school
in a silver wheelchair, and she let the kids
push her around in it. And some of them
sat in her lap as she read to them
at reading time. And they asked her
questions, unselfconsciously, the way
only kids will ask: What happened
to your legs? Where are the legs now?
How do you take a shower? How
do you drive a car? It was not unlike
show-and-tell, and my Aunt Hannah
was happy to answer. She even joked a little,
and slapped one stump and then the other,
so it looked like a flam on a pair of bongos,
or a rim shot after the punch line
of a bad joke in the Catskills.

Throwing Snowballs at Cars

From our little redoubt
up on the hill
we lobbed our redoubtable

arsenal of white
handcrafted ordnance
one by one over the hedges

and listened
for the gratifying
thunk

on the roofs and hoods of the passing
innocents
who mostly just kept trundling dumbly

along
through the purely perfect-for-packing
driven snow. But once

an innocent in a beat-up pickup
stopped. And stayed there. Idling. Fuming.
We froze. Our fingers and toes

twitching. Our hearts racing. Our noses
running. Finally he drove off, but he doubled
back around, and routed our little

redoubt. And there's no doubt
he would have beaten the shit out of us
if he caught any of us—

but we dispersed
like a burst snowball ourselves
and melted into the neighborhood

like so many scared shitless
snowflakes, no two of us exactly
repentant.

Fledgling

My training wheels lie in the grass
like legs. My father stands over them,
steadying the bicycle with one hand
while with the other he beckons
with a grimy finger. A Phillips-head
sticks in the earth beside the severed
pair. The whole scene looks like an amputation.
I will never walk again, if I can help it—
as soon as I learn how to fly. Flying
will be a little like dying, and a little
like being born. I mount the bike
which wobbles slightly in my father's grip
the way the earth wobbles in the grip
of the late afternoon sun going down
behind the huddled houses. The seat
which is a little higher than the sun,
and the handlebars which are approximately
two stars, together form my north and south poles.
My spine is the prime meridian. My nose
sticks out over the top of the hill, on top
of the world, sniffing the air for the bottom.

Foreclosure

We took it out back
and we beat the stuffing out of it,
then we stuffed it, broken, into the back
of the car, and dumped its mutilated body at the dump.
It felt good to do this. After all, the cat had peed on it twice,
and the mortgage company had sent another threatening letter,
and we felt like kicking the shit out of some bankers—
but all we could do was sit back down
on the couch, and drink another beer,
and our helplessness smacked of
cat piss.

So we dragged it outside
and bludgeoned it with the sledgehammer.
Then we took the ax to its back, its arms and legs
and middle, the springs coiled up inside like large and small
intestines spilling out in the yard as we chopped and hacked,
breathing hard from the hard work of beating
the crap out of something you might have
caressed in another life, or another
house, one without a cat with
a urinary tract infection,
or one without

an adjustable rate mortgage,
an ARM you want to break but can't—
so you look around for something else to break,
and it could be your banker or it could be your cat or it could be
someone you loved in another life, or maybe even in this life.
And it feels good to do this. But then it begins
to feel like an indiscretion. And then
like a desecration. And then
it begins. Like a death.
A death with its own
life.

The Man Reading His Checkbook

is turning the pages over painstakingly
as though he were trying to balance
the world
on the short line
of the long autobiographical poem
he's been working on his whole
working life—
this teetering, accreting
catalog worthy of Walt Whitman
with room enough for everything
from the groceries to the proctologist's co-pay
to Subaru to the Hartford Federal
Mortgage Company to Dee Dee's
company. "It's nothing personal," she purrs,
"but I don't take personal checks," her eyes
apologizing. That's when he takes out his wallet
which is just a different version
of the same poem, full of doubts
and imminences, and exquisitely
poignant sections which would
make you cry—and reads through it once,
silently to himself, then offers it up to her
like a thing he can't afford
not to take back.

Construction Site

I-beams remind me
of the first person.
And the second person.
I love the bones of you.
Look at that building going up across the street:
the construction workers have spray-painted
Esther, Kate, Delilah, Meg,
Rhonda, Cherisse, Chantelle, Sue—
all up and down and across
the huge I-beams of their magnificent
work in progress. *Julia, Lucretia,*
Veronica, Eve, Heidi, Cassandra,
Sonya, Ruth—the names of so many
women and girls (and also a few
men—*Fong, Steve, Hugh*)
at the heart of so many life stories.
And after the concrete gets poured
and the sheetrock goes up
and the carpeting goes down
and all the doors get hung,
those names will be in there
forever, written on the very
rib of the creation.

Schadenfreude

"Leave it to the Germans," said Ben.
"They didn't invent it," I said. "They just named it."
"To name a thing is to own it," he said. "It's theirs."
And he walked away then,

waving goodbye with his
back to me, airily, triumphantly, the argument
won, the conversation over as
far as he was concerned. Though I don't

dislike Ben exactly, nor envy him his
wife or Ph.D., which is in poetry—
the wife very pretty, beautiful even—when
a month later he tells me she told him she wants

out, I can't help feeling—not joy
exactly, I wouldn't call it *Freude*—
not the sort of feeling you'd write an ode to,
but more the sort you might

write a dark little conversational piece
in quatrains about—
just to say the conversation isn't over
until it's over.

Question

If a man falls to his knees in a forest
and there's nobody there to hear
his soft weeping
and the trees are all standing around
not doing anything
and the animals have turned
back to what is their own
and the insects are loitering in the doorways
of his eyes and ears and nostrils
rubbing their hands together with
gusto

does it make
sense to sing happy birthday
in a room with noisemakers and conical hats
and streamers and balloons above a white table
where a man is sitting
weeping on his knees in a forest
like dysentery among the desserts
like the suicide hanging
beside a burst piñata
the laughter and shrieks of children
mixing with birdsong?

That

After that he lost his sense of humor.
It wasn't that nothing was funny.
It was just that that wasn't funny.
It was just that. That and a world that
could allow that to happen. Nothing
funny in the world after that. Before that
everything funny in the world was only funny
because that hadn't happened yet. And yet
it had happened, and it had been happening
in the world ever since the world had
begun. How to reconcile that was
the question. How in the world to
laugh with that in the world? That was
the riddle, the conundrum whose answer
was once a clever pun, but now was just
this bruised silence, this dumb twitching,
this tongue cut right out.

Pleasure

When you're in pain
you take
pleasure in nothing
but pain's
diminishment,
if pleasure
you can call it,
testing
the thinness of it,
disbelieving,
distrusting,
tiptoeing
down into the kitchen
where a few dirty dishes
that aren't yours
wait in the sink,
and you begin
washing them
slowly,
thoroughly,
gratefully,
the warm
water on your wrists,
the sweet-
smelling soap, the clean
dishes stacking
in the dish rack,
dripping,
glistening,
solid.

Phoenix

Too sick for words
the monks
invented a way
with the hands
to make the first letter only
of the prayers
they wanted to recite but couldn't
from their burning
sickbeds
in the fourteenth
century

and these handshapes
each representing a whole
passage
lifted up to God who
knew the words by heart
anyway and only
needed a hand
a finger really
to point Him
in the direction
of an intention

rose up like smoke
from the burning
sickbeds of the monks
up through the chimneys
of the centuries
and turned into
the birds that build their nests
in the hands of the deaf
flitting and darting from sleeve
to sleeve where they still
sing to this day

Long Battle with Cancer

What he needed was a little more patriotism,
a little more fight, a little more fuckin' A
for kicking cancer's butt. But the thing was,
he was a conscript. His heart wasn't in it,
whereas these volunteers, these mercenaries—
these doctors and nurses and radiologists
and radiation oncologists who made their living
killing cancer—their hearts were in it; they were
into the good fight. But his heart, for its part,
was set on desertion. And so he kept on looking
out the window of the transport vehicle
at the trees swishing by en route to the appointed
appointments. He kept on looking for a way
out. A way to escape into the trees, disappear
into the woods, then surface in some neutral country
where life was going on as usual and nobody
cared or talked about or paid any attention at all
to this tiresome old war that was still going on
inside him. But there was no neutral country,
no such place; no village, house, room, corner
of the world where the long battle he could bet
his life that his obit would reference, wasn't going on.

Oath

Being sick I swear I will
seek out other sick people,
the fellowship of the sick
which heals me of the eyes
of the healthy, the terrible
hope of loved ones, the lies
that melt on the tongues
whose excellent appetites
and singing glottises
and vibrating tongue rings
do not belong to me.
I will make of my leper's bell
a symphony of bells. I will
take my bacterium
to the bacterial dance floor,
and do the bug, the viral,
the metastasis, the funky
microbial. I will shake my legs
like a tick who has found
the deer-throat of love.
Being sick I will be sick
unapologetically, and with
abandon, and with someone
else who is also sick with
all his heart and all his soul.

Escape Artist

I've always wanted to be
excused. From the table.
From school. From work.
From life, actually.
I don't feel well, may I be
excused from feeling?
I've always wanted to get
out of things. Downright
Houdiniesque. I'd like
to get out of this body. I don't
remember how I got in.
I'd like to go by climbing
your body. Down your body and out
of my body. I think that's how
we get here in the first place.
I don't remember the first place.
I'd like to go back there though.
Excuse me if I elbow,
shoulder, knee. Excuse me if I
worm my way out of the crowded
now. We either go by breaking
into blossom, or by wilting
in place, the latter being so
heartbreaking, you have to look
away. You have to look away.

Note

All I need is a car
and some gas
and a garage, and I'm good to go. Good
to go. To cease upon the midnight with no pain.
Half in love with easeful death
all my life. All my life I have
been jumping to death the way others
jump to other conclusions. When I got sick
I jumped to my death. When I fell in love
I said, "She is so
beautiful I want to die." But a suicide
isn't born a suicide.
He wasn't a suicide in elementary school.
And he wasn't a suicide in band practice.
And he wasn't a suicide when he was playing left field.
For a long time he just wanted to be
one of those words that are acts.
A speech act. To say one is to do it. To actually
do it. I *promise*. I *apologize*. Maybe that's why
he was always making promises,
and always apologizing
for breaking them. To cease upon
the midnight with no pain,
no pain being the operative
words here. For he doth hate pain. You can
operate a garage door from the front seat,
close it with the electric garage door opener
while your car is still running, and not get out,
and not walk back into your life.
You can sit there thinking about
the lines in certain poems
while the car is singing soft and low
and Lethe-wards. Being
too happy in thine happiness.

I don't think I've ever been
too happy in mine or anyone else's happiness.
Maybe that's why I'm sitting here now
all alone except for the sleds and the bicycles
and the lawnmower and the snow shovels
and garbage bins, thinking about Keats and
tuberculosis. And wondering: if *he* had a car
and some gas, and a garage, would he
have done what he said in that poem?
I know the words are not the act itself.
These words are coming before the act.
After the act, others will come
and read these words, looking for reasons.
I *apologize.* To the living.
I know the act itself says
there is no reason to go on living.
I know it's kind of a slap in the face.
But it's nothing personal.
I wasn't talking about your
life when I took my own.
Your life is still beautiful in so many
words. I *love* you is another
one of those words, you could say.
Or you could argue that it isn't.

People in Deaf Houses

Here's the church and here's the steeple.
The deaf people have barricaded the doors,
hot-wired the school buses, moved them
in front of the gates, and let the air out of the tires.
They've shut the campus down, and the police
can't do anything about it, because they don't
know sign language. And neither does the president
of the college. And neither does the chairman of the board
of trustees, and neither do the trustees themselves.
The trustees can't be trusted with this college, this
church, this school, this blessed sacrament.

In the deaf world, deaf is good. Deaf people marry
other deaf people, and live in deaf houses,
and do not throw deaf carpenters' telephone numbers
away, but give them to other deaf homeowners
looking for a good deaf carpenter, because deaf
is a good and trusted name all over the deaf world.

Here's the hospital and here's the urology unit.
Open the door and see all the doctors
with their deft fingers and expensive educations.
Here is one performing a vasectomy
on a deaf patient who has elected to have it
because he doesn't want any children.
And the surgeon has a slight accent, maybe
German. And the sign language interpreter
has a professional code of ethics,
and is signing what the surgeon is saying
but not what the interpreter is thinking
about German-speaking surgeons and vasectomies,
about Aryans and eugenicists and the forced
sterilizations of the congenitally deaf
in Europe only 40 years ago, about the protests

going on right now at Gallaudet, and about
cochlear implants being performed in this very
hospital, on deaf children who haven't elected to have them.

Alexander Graham Bell invented the telephone.
He was a teacher of the deaf. He had a deaf mother,
and a deaf wife, too. And he knew
that deaf people marry other deaf people
and live in deaf houses. And he deplored that fact.
He deplored deaf people. He urged Congress to act,
to prohibit deaf marriages, to reduce the risk
of more deaf babies. He wasn't a Hitler
or an Eichmann exactly. He didn't advocate
killing the deaf. He loved the deaf. He taught the deaf.
He was only trying to eradicate the deaf
for their own good. For the good of the world.

Here's the church and here's
the steeple. The deaf students are burning
their oppressors in effigy. They're saying: *Look!*
To anyone with eyes to see, they're saying: *Look!*
And the interpreter's fingers are flying,
and the surgeon's fingers are snipping, and the nurse is
adjusting the light above the deaf patient
lying on the table with his johnny hiked up, his little
deaf penis the center of attention. And the interpreter
who has been trying all this time not to look at it,
looks at it. Takes a good long look.

Leveling the Playing Field

Before they leveled the playing field
one side was always running uphill,
which was hard. And the other side
was always running downhill, which was
hard too—hard to stop the ball from rolling,
hard to stop yourself from running
when you're running down a hill after a ball.
Downhill had certain advantages though.
It was true. But uphill had advantages too—
you could belay; you could stick a strategic
foot out, trip a careening downhill guy
mid-stride. And anyway, we usually
switched at halftime. So when the referees
came up with the idea, we scratched our heads
and tried to envision a playing field that was
level. "You mean get rid of the hill?" we asked
incredulously. They nodded vehemently
and their excellent silver whistles hanging
on lanyards 'round their necks bobbed in sympathy.
The bulldozers and the backhoes arrived
the next day, the tines of their buckets biting
into our hill, eating it away before our eyes,
and before we could say time out, or foul play,
or off sides—which some of us did say, although
by then it was too late—they'd gone and changed
the game forever. Some of us quit outright, preferring
to sit in judgment up in the stands—the closest
thing to a hill that they had. And some of us kept on playing,
adapting ourselves to the changing landscape,
learning the new steps, and the new names, making
new friends, many of whom were so young that
they'd never played on a hill. They could only
imagine, they said. They could only shake their heads
and regard us in a squinting sort of way, as though
the sun were going down behind a hill, behind us.

Geographic Tongue

My daughter wants to see the world.
She's nineteen and fearless.
I wrestled Marc Silva in the 8th grade.
He threw me down on the mat
and pinned me in thirty seconds.
"Those red lesions on your left dorsal
look a little suspicious," my dentist said.

She will go to Mexico, Guatemala,
Colombia and Brazil.
Silva's biceps were thigh-thick.
He flexed them and they sang.
My mother loved Edith Piaf. "Robert
Zimmerman is an excellent oral surgeon
with an office in Norwood," my dentist said.

"It's also Bob Dylan's real name," I said.
Then I waited a month for an appointment,
during which time I developed cancer
of the mouth and esophagus, in my head.
Piaf is French for "little sparrow." Tongue
is the strongest muscle in the human body.
Silva is the most common surname in Brazil.

Everything turns out fine. She ends up
marrying a man twenty years her junior.
He invites me to his house to lift weights.
She dances through the drug wars
like hopscotch. He says they're just fissures.
Which sounds like fishers. Dorsal fins.
Fishers of men. Jesus. *Je ne regrette rien.*

The Grace of the French Horn

for Eric R.

My name is Eric and I'm an addict.
Grace was a kind of deviating, a kind of diverging,
a kind of mistake. It was wholly undeserved,
wholly unexpected, wholly perfect.

I do not perceive my own best interests.
For example, I'd have picked the trumpet.
I really wanted to play the trumpet,
but in fourth grade they were giving out the instruments

alphabetically, and by the time they got to the Rs
the trumpets were all gone. I remember
picking through what was left, that sad remainder,
wondering if they had any electric guitars

stashed away in a backroom somewhere. Grace
was my place in the alphabet in elementary school,
accounting for a choice that's unaccountable:
that horn with the large intestine, the only brass

left on the table, and the closest thing
to a trumpet that they had.
I'll trade up for a trumpet in fifth grade,
I thought. Grace was what foiled my own best thinking.

For I picked it up by the flaring bell, held it to my ear,
and peered inside—I was only eight—
and I haven't put it down since, except to eat,
sleep, and twice to marry.

By age nineteen, I was principal horn
with the Cleveland Orchestra. By twenty-one,
I'd played in London, Paris, Prague, Rome,
Shanghai, Sidney, Seoul. Then one morning

around 2 a.m., I put my French horn down
to smoke cocaine for the first time. A love affair
from the get-go. Seems I had a flair
for the technique, had it down

before I picked it up. Here were the same
hand positions, on a smaller scale:
the bell hand held the bowl,
the fingering hand fingered the match, the flame

flared, stuttered, and danced as the lights
flickered and I breathed in deep, held it, held it, held it—
my lungs were made for this. For all the world
I blew the blue-black smoke out, night after night

after night. Year after year. The French horn is a curving
into circles of a great unmanageable length. I sold
my horn one night for the next hit. My soul
died in that vicious circle. Grace was a swerving.

Time & Money

With difficulty you produce your voluminous wallet
and the girl behind the counter takes a deep breath.
The line behind you swells. The wallet just sits there
on the counter obscenely, half-open, like an obese drunk
exposing himself or herself to you and the girl who says
eww. You dip two fingers, then a third, into the vagina-like
folds of the wallet and rummage around for the required
item. This seems to take a very long time. So long, in fact,
that you have forgotten what the required item is, the girl
has grown very old, the line behind you has withered
on the vine and fallen off, and finally a blue library card
falls out, and a ticket to the Gardner Museum, a flurry
of band-aids, several bills, some coins, a yellowed corner
of napkin with a girl's name and phone number on it. Could it
be *this* girl's phone number, you wonder, the pointy teeth
of a spare key kissing your fingertips somewhere deep inside
the reaches of your wallet. You fish out the key and offer it
to the girl. Her old, mottled, gnarled hand, which is beautiful
in a way you never thought of as beautiful, closes around
the key, with its promise, its heft, its glinting mountainous teeth.

Fold This Poem in Half

Fold this poem in half.
Now fold it in half again,
and again. Notice how,
if you did it right, it fits
on an eighth of the page,
the way the moon fits
in the backseat window
of the car traveling through
the night, the road unfolding
like a story from childhood,
the white space surrounding
the poem collapsed like time
into this one moment reflected
in a little corner of the sky.

Courtship Dives of the Male Hummingbird

He pretends he doesn't see her.
She pretends she doesn't see him.
But they have noticed each other.
They are both so small in the world.
How in the world will they ever meet?
She has no idea. But he has an idea.
It's one of those crazy great ideas
men get when they're in love.
The kind that just might work.
The kind that makes a man great
and gets him the woman. The world
is full of crazy great ideas, and this one
belongs to the male hummingbird. He will
dive-bomb at 58.6 miles per hour
with a body drag coefficient of 0.3,
as if to say, "Because you don't have eyes for me
I'm going to have to kill myself."
Then out of the corner of his eye
he checks to see if she looks concerned. And when
it looks like he's going to crash and burn,
she does. And then he knows. And then his heart
leaps up, and he pulls up at the last second
with a centripetal acceleration that
is rivaled only by the best jet fighter pilots.
Then he banks, and jukes, and flits back down
to earth, and takes her out for a drink of nectar.

Multi-Purpose Room

We could all say "multi-purpose room"
already by the time we were 7 or 8.
It's one of those words that has remained
buried deep inside my childhood until
now. Like "filmstrip" and "recess" and
"writing utensil." I want to say something about
the things I used to say in elementary school,
like "I'll be your best friend" and "I have
to stay after" and "she stuffs." Where did I
learn to say so crass and demeaning a thing
as "she stuffs"? Probably in the multi-purpose room
during gym class, or during a school dance
or a school play, or the Pinewood Derby. Maybe
it was when the school photographer came
with his cameras and tripod and flash bulbs
and complimentary black combs and we all
filed down to the multi-purpose room to get
our pictures taken up on the stage—the boys
with their jackets and ties or turtlenecks,
the girls with their dresses and bows
and beautiful long hair falling down over
the borders of the developing countries
of their bodies, of which we boys were foreign
observers. Back then our own bodies were
as different from theirs, ecologically speaking,
as deserts from rainforests. What made us think
we were qualified to judge the nature of
that growth, when most of us hadn't even
one slender tendril going in any of the nether
regions, regions which would one day boast
multi-purposes of their own, which we neither
dreamt of yet, nor understood at all. But that
didn't stop us from acting like we did, up
on that stage, before that thick green curtain.

Social Studies

He's off to fight
the Punic Wars
for Carthage

which lost all three.
He loves the underdog.
He has an angle:

he's getting all dressed up
as Hannibal
to give his book report today

in 6th grade
social studies class.
A is for Alps.

"Punic"
is derived from *Poeni,*
the Roman name

for the Phoenicians,
or Carthaginians.
He straightens

his facts,
kisses his elephant-
emblazoned cardboard shield

for good luck,
flourishes
his aluminum foil sword, and steps

out of my Toyota Elephant
squeezed in among the yellow
school busses.

O my Hannibal,
I would teach you
that all the puffing up

in the history of the world
so far
has amounted

to a pimple
on the rear end
of a back-row

6th grader—
today's victorious
Roman in your

homeroom tomorrow,
asking to borrow
a pencil.

Homophobia

I have a friend who is hydrophobic—
he wants to learn how to swim
but he is too afraid
of the water
to give himself over to it
and just float.

And I have another friend who
is agoraphobic—he wants
to see the world,
and to see the country,
and to see the big city,
but he's too afraid
to come out
of his tiny apartment
which is a closet really.

And my claustrophobic friend would love
to take the elevator,
my gephyrophobic friend wishes
she could drive over bridges
instead of having to go all the way around
each morning to get to work
and each night to get home again
before finally lying down
next to the one she loves.

Bridge & Main

I am in love with the man
who let me in
in traffic this morning
with a silent arpeggio
above his steering wheel

signaling me to enter
where he waited
and all that huddled humanity
balked and steamed
in a long line behind him

snaking all the way back
to where I imagine
he came from—
Bellingham or Mendon
or Providence—

I am in love with the eternal
feminine in the man
who lets me
in the ways
of the world.

How to Touch a Woman

Technically and with a love of
technicalities mixed with childlike
wonder, and also a little shame
at the long history of the ignorance
of men. Touch her the way
you would touch whatever's behind
glass and a "Do Not Touch" sign
if the glass were suddenly removed
and the sign were given to you
to fold into a beautiful paper crane
to give to her. Touch her that way
every time as though it were
the first time. And when you consider
your cells and her cells are dying
and being born all the time, technically it is.

My Mother's Whitman

which is my Whitman now
sits on my shelf
reclines actually
horizontally
displaying its spine
above the spines
of ten or twenty
younger slenderer poets
and it's almost
sexual the way
he's in them
unquestionably
his influence
all over them

the way my mother
who never remarried
after my father died
never dated never
kissed another man or
woman on the mouth
for twenty long years
then died herself
still beautiful in
her early sixties
is in my voice
and in my hunger
and in my reticence
which is her reticence.

Honda Pavarotti

after Hoagland

My Aunt Hannah loved Pavarotti
so when she came to Boston for the second
opinion on the leg, he was belting it out
on the tape deck in my car parked live
outside the diabetes hospital. Live parking
is when your body waits in your car
the way a soul waits in a body idling
in a hospital. And when the doctor said
she would have to lose the leg or else
we would surely lose Aunt Hannah and that
was his expert opinion for which he surely
would charge an arm and a leg, she looked
like a book you can't read because it's closed
and leaning its stiff and fraying spine against
the closed book of your cousin walking slowly
beside her toward your car. So what I did was
I cranked up the volume because I knew
my Aunt Hannah loved Pavarotti, but after
she'd lowered the wreck-in-progress of her
body into the front seat, she angrily clicked
the music off. And the aria died right there
in the dead air of my car. So I put it in drive
and went screeching out of there without a word.

One-and-Twenty

When I was fifty-one with that kind of insomnia
where you wake up earlier and earlier
and drink lots of coffee and write
lots of poetry, my son was just nineteen
with that home-from-college-for-the-summer
kind of mania, where you go to bed later
and later, and sleep until two in the afternoon.
The drinking age in America was one-and-twenty.
A. E. Housman was a classical scholar
who wrote lots of poetry about doomed youth
in the English countryside. No use talking
to a lad of nineteen about waiting two years
before starting to drink, especially when
he's already learned how up in college. Housman
taught at a college in London, and later at a college
in Cambridge. One night we passed each other—me
and the lad—like two sleepless ship captains in a dark
kitchen at four in the morning. I was heading
for the coffee. He was heading for the toilet.
I could smell the booze on his breath from across
the ages. "Dad," he said, "I can't believe you
get up this early—what time is it, anyway?"
"Son," I said, like a refrain, "I can't believe you
are getting home this late. It's four o'clock in the morning!"
Then we both sailed silently on in our opposite
directions, with our opposite wakes. But a few
minutes later, sipping my coffee and scratching
out a line, then putting it back again, I sensed him
hovering tipsily in the doorway, steeply rocking.
"I love you, man," he said, a little drunkenly.
And I knew enough of love, and I knew enough
of poetry, and I knew enough of sobriety to know
he meant it more than he could say sober. "I love you, too,
man," I said, gave the boy a kiss, and put him to bed.

Dear Hallmark

I know some kids who'd rather make their own.
And I know some grownups who would rather
cut their own tongues out
than let you speak for them. Helplessly intelligent
surrealists, glib intellectuals, haiku bicyclists, some
of my best friends. But I'll give you this, you have
sold more poems than all the moderns and postmoderns
put together. And the people love you. Are the people just
stupid? Are the poets just jealous? Are the pharmacists
just high on life? The truth is, I love your timeless
earnestness. I do. In sickness and in health. Births and deaths
and all occasions in between. Because it goes without saying—
the whole world goes without saying. Saying doesn't
make it go. Never did and never will. But you,
you say without going, like the clock that doesn't
go, the clock that stays the same, your hands always
together, in applause, or prayer, or shared joy, or sorrow where
you can only wring your hands, fumble for the words,
and say the words are inadequate. Which, of course, they are.
But at least you say them. You say them for us when we go
without saying, and when we go without knowing
what to say, or don't go at all but send you stammering
in our stead. And here I stand in your aisle, in your
shadow, in your presence, my hands in my pockets, fumbling
for my wallet, feeling like I'm in the presence of
not greatness, not brilliance, not scholarship or virtuosity,
but love. I am in the presence of love here, helplessly
simple, deliberately compassionate, practicing forever
its imperfect loopy cursive with its pink tongue sticking out.

Hegemony

Three of my cousins are deaf.
But I have lots of cousins,
so the deaf ones
were always in the minority
at family gatherings
where they'd commandeer a couch
or the kitchen table and juggle
their hands. It was a language
the rest of us didn't understand
because we never bothered to learn it.
Their conversations and our conversations
sailed along contiguously
like ships passing in the night
or like an English frigate passing
over a Deaf submarine during
détente. One by one they got married
to three deaf spouses. So then there were six.
And one of them ended up having
two deaf children. So then there were eight.
Eventually they all divorced
and remarried other deaf people
with deaf stepchildren and deaf exes
and deaf in-laws and deaf
cousins. And before we knew it
we were totally outnumbered
at the family gatherings
and consigned to a corner
of the sectional, whispering
and ducking the flying hands,
feeling rather small
and blind, like moles or voles
trembling in the shadows
of the raptors.

Half Moon

The two chairs
that we sat in

this morning
in our pajamas

in the sunny
kitchen

kissing

are still in the same
position

this evening
when I get home

in the dark
I sit in

one
then the other

Her Ear

He loved her ear
literally. Not
the figurative ear—
not the sensitivity
to music or poetry
which she arguably
didn't possess—
but her literal ear.
Its pinna and lobe.
Its cartilaginous-
ness. He loved
to take it in his mouth
and bite it tenderly,
lovingly. And he loved
looking into her brown eyes
which took the world in
literally, and shone
with a happiness
that was brown as earth
with flecks of green.

Passive Voice

It is given to me
is the passive they're parsing
in linguistics class.

He's the sign language interpreter
for a deaf student making
eyes at him

and noise with her corn chips'
plastic wrapper.
She's tonguing a corn chip

and wrinkling her nose
which she knows he knows
means *ooh salty,*

and telling him in
no uncertain terms,
It is given to you.

Sometimes it happens
that way: love
just lands in your lap,

starts conjugating itself
in the second person
singular.

He will ask her to marry him,
to give up linguistics,
come live with him in

a house in the suburbs
among the "Thickly
Settled" signs.

Here's the church
and here's the steeple.
The deaf people will sit

where they can see
the sign language interpreter.
They will name their first child

Vowel, after
the dilating mouth
of pleasure,

fill their home
with the tongues of a hundred
speechless lives:

the plosives of fish
browsing the fishbowl,
the shrugging shoulders

of the spider plants,
the noiseless stutter
of candles.

It's all just tremblingly
achingly waiting
to be

received.

Pigeon Lady

"For me they are like the tide,"
says the pigeon lady, and I've a thought
she's keeping one inside—

a rainbow-necked, red-eyed,
pinioned pigeon weeps in her throat:
"For me they are like the tide—

a thousand times I've tried
to wet my fingers, to touch.
But retreating, they keep inside

each other's little struts, they nod
and float away, nod and float
away. For me they are like the tide."

Behind her drizzling side-
long frowns and crumbs the sun is out.
She's keeping one inside

like that feather lodged or tied
in her blue-gray hair, it's there. It can't hide.
"For me they are like the tide."
Cheeping, one's inside.

Scrabble with Amber

Zet isn't a word.
    Yes it is.
And you can't go diagonal.
    Yes I can.

Eight-year-old Amber
    is my girlfriend's daughter.
She isn't my daughter.
    Yet she is.

Because we all live together
    in the same house—
Amber, her brother, her mother,
    the two cats, a rabbit,

hamster and me—
    trying to make
something of it. Do you have
    an A? *Zeta* is the sixth letter

of the Greek alphabet.
    No it's not. And anyway
I don't have an A. And you're not
    the boss of me.

Light Bulb

"I wanna be an inventor
like Thomas Lava Edison," he says,
erupting from the dinner table
and trailing a white dinner napkin

and leaving his untouched mashed potatoes
in the shape of a volcano,
the gravy cooling inside the crater
left by the beaked ladle.

After the chuckling dishwasher dies down
I press my ear to the door of his
laboratory, and I hear his small voice
asking questions and also

answering. Soon he reappears with
two toy cars, a red one and a blue,
parks them on the dining room table,
installs himself in a chair—my chair—

and bids me sit. The demonstration begins:
"I've invented a talking car horn, Dad.
With a menu. You choose from the things *you* always say
when people cut you off, or move too slow,

or don't put on their blinkers. Only *now*
they'll be able to hear you." The cars start up:
VROOM, VROOM. The red one shouts:
"Come on, wake up, buddy. Sometime this

century would be nice." The blue replies: "Relax,"
and turns left. The red continues straight: "Nice
turn signal, jerk." He looks up at me with
eyes as big as headlights. "Would you

buy it?" he asks as the cars fly up
and out in opposite arcs above his head,
grind to a halt midair, upside down in his hands.

Salamanders

We can't believe it's the first
time I'm seeing one in fifty-three years
on the planet, Josh who is ten
and a collector, a connoisseur
of salamanders, and me his late-
middle-aged step-dad. "They live
on every continent except Antarctica,"
he says, holding it up to my nose for a better
first look at this two-inch worm with a head
and arms and legs, and, incredibly,
fingers and toes, that he found
under a rock this morning. And I think
I have been living under a rock myself—
the wrong rock—because I've never
seen one of these little miracles
with digits before. Or maybe I did
and I just don't remember because
there was no one around like Josh
holding it up to my nose in the shared
cup of his own amazement. I think we
learn to love this world from those who
loved the world before us, but sometimes—
especially lately—those are the ones who
have come after us, reaching up to touch
our shoulder, saying, *Look at this miraculous*
living thing I am holding in my hands
and you are holding in your hands, too.

Letting Go

This is a required poem.
You do not have to read it now.
You can wait until
you're dying if you want to.
But you have to let go of everything.
You have to let go of everything.
You can start by letting go
of this poem. Just let it
go. Let it fall to the desk, skim
the edge, spill to the floor. Let it
lie on the floor face-down
so you can't read it. How
to read this poem when
it's lying on the floor face-down
like a body?
That is the seeming difficulty
of this poem. On the one side
words are everything. On the other
nothing. Just the poem saying
to let it go on without you. Saying
on the other side there's nothing
as difficult as it seems.

Acknowledgments

Thanks to the following magazines and journals in which many of these poems, often in earlier versions, previously appeared.

Baltimore Review, Barefoot Review, Blood Root, Burnt District, Centrifugal Eye, Common Ground Review, Clerc Scar, The Chimaera, cur.ren.cy, Diode, Dos Passos Review, Earth's Daughters, Evening Street Review, Exercise Bowler, Fear of Monkeys, Extracts, FutureCycle, Gloom Cupboard, Hospital Drive, Hyperlexia Journal, J Journal, Mad Swirl, Naugatuck River Review, Negative Suck, Off the Coast, Paper Nautilus, Penny Ante Feud, Pirene's Fountain, Poetica, Poets Online, Protest Poems, Pure Francis, Right Hand Pointing, r.kv.r.y., Science Poetry, Shortpoem.org, Snail Mail Review, Sein und Werden, Solstice Literary Magazine, Straight Forward Poetry, Terrain.org, Thick with Conviction, 10x3Plus, Third Wednesday, Toasted Cheese, Umbrella, Vox Poetica, Wild Goose Poetry Review, Wordgathering, Work to a Calm

Photo of the author by Christine O'Reilly; cover and book design by Diane Kistner, dkistner@futurecycle.org; book set in DejaVu Serif with Diavlo Bold titling.

About FutureCycle Press

FutureCycle Press is dedicated to publishing lasting English-language poetry and flash fiction books, chapbooks, and anthologies in both print-on-demand and ebook formats. Founded in 2007 by long-time independent editor/publishers and partners Diane Kistner and Robert S. King, the press incorporated as a nonprofit in 2012. A number of our editors are distinguished poets and authors in their own right, and we have been actively involved in the small press movement going back to the early seventies.

Our annual anthology, *FutureCycle*, combines poetry and flash fiction. The FutureCycle Poetry Book Prize and honorarium is awarded annually for the best full-length volume of poetry we publish in a calendar year. We are dedicated to giving all authors we publish the care their work deserves, making our catalog of titles the most distinguished it can be, and paying forward any earnings to fund more great books.

We've learned a few things about independent publishing over the years. We've also evolved a unique, resilient publishing model that allows us to focus mainly on vetting and preserving for posterity the most books of exceptional quality without becoming overwhelmed with bookkeeping and mailing, fundraising activities, or taxing editorial and production "bubbles." To find out more about what we are doing, come see us at www.futurecycle.org.

www.ingramcontent.com/pod-product-compliance
Lightning Source LLC
LaVergne TN
LVHW051804080426
835511LV00019B/3404